If You Can Look Up, You Can Get Up

Daily Principles for Keeping Victory
Each Day of Your Life

Byron C. Hayes, Ph. D.

authorHOUSE®

AuthorHouse™
1663 Liberty Drive
Bloomington, IN 47403
www.authorhouse.com
Phone: 1-800-839-8640

© 2010 Byron C. Hayes, Ph. D.. All rights reserved.

No part of this book may be reproduced, stored in a retrieval system, or transmitted by any means without the written permission of the author.

First published by AuthorHouse 3/12/2010

ISBN: 978-1-4490-6953-7 (e)
ISBN: 978-1-4490-6957-5 (sc)

Library of Congress Control Number: 2010900109

Printed in the United States of America
Bloomington, Indiana

This book is printed on acid-free paper.

INTRODUCTION

Hello, my name is Jason Hayes. I am a firm believer that in order to reach our horizons in life, there must be balance. If you are a consultant, entrepreneur, investor, broker, stock holder, banker, CEO, public school teacher, physician, attorney, state judge, gymnast, law enforcer, fire fighter, white or blue collar worker, stay at home mom, etc., motivation is the key to directing everyday life with all of its ups and downs. Do not forget the brush fires in life, and we face many of them!

My dad, Dr. Byron C. Hayes, believes that in spite of it all, "If we can look up, we can get up!" Life is an ongoing battle faced by fear, panic, emotion, stress, family trauma and job downsizing. But because we are GOD believers, word trusters, and faith walkers, we have learned to stay motivated, and we score a victory every time. We have learned that when life hands us lemons, we are to make lemonade and when life hands us a bowl of cherries, we must overcome the pits. In this life-changing book, you will receive a step-by-step, day-by-day victory approach to reach the place called there in our lives. Remember, it is not over until we win, for I John 4:4 reads:

"Ye are of God, little children, and have overcome them, because greater is he that is in you, than he that is in the world."

As Dr. Hayes' son, I have grown up with many of these wisdom and motivational principles. It is through these and the word of GOD that my life is placed on course. My dad has always said that it is too soon to quit and there is no time for stopping.
Galatians 5:7 reads:

"Ye did run well; who did hinder you that ye should not obey the truth?"

All scripture references in this book are from the King James Version of the Bible. My mother and father brought me up on the King James Version. It is that Bible that has changed my life and set me on course. Although some biblical references in this book may be revised, it is only for clarification. Dr. Hayes is a firm believer that repetition is the mother of learning. You will find that at times, my father will repeat the same motivational principle. This is so that it will register and add more impact to your life.

While going through this book and allowing it to change your life, you may say to yourself, "I would love for Dr. Hayes to come and speak at my conferences, church, men's group, ladies' group, etc." You can contact Dr. Hayes by calling (989) 752-1675 or by emailing at wofim@aol.com. You may also write us at Word of Faith International Ministries, Attn: Dr. Byron C. Hayes, 500 N. Washington Avenue, PO Box 14751, Saginaw, MI 48601.

So, I pray that you will be blessed as you read my dad's book. Always remember, and I say as my dad says, **"If You Can Look Up, You Can Get Up!"**
Jason C. Hayes

Chapter 1
Your best days are ahead

Your best days are ahead the moment you begin to read this book. This is your day for the victory that you have been waiting for. Your sun is peaking over the clouds of your life. Your rain is drying up from your latest storm. You are starting to wake up! Even now your tears of pain will start turning into tears of joy. For **Psalms 118:24** reads, *"This is the day that the Lord has made."*

How many people have stolen your victory? How many people have stolen your testimony, your joy, your praise, your miracles, your faith, your dreams, your freedom, your esteem, your decision making, your character, your personality, and your identity? Well, now is the time to break free from the robbers of your past. We must learn to press pass pressure. Faith says:

- **Let that worry go and live**
- **Worry is a dreadful disease**
- **Worry is a slow eating cancer**
- **Worry will make you sick and weakly**
- **Worry is a waste of energy**
- **Worry will wear you out**
- **Worry will take your sleep**
- **Worry will steal your joy**

Don't worry about anything; **pray** about everything. Keep your eyes off the problem and fixed on GOD.

In the body of Christ, so many are losing the faith. Satan has become a deadly force bringing worry all over the nation. Worry is a lie from the enemy. Worry ties GOD's hands. Worry raises the blood pressure and stress level. Worry causes heart problems.

Jesus said in **St. John 10:10,** "The thief cometh not, but for to steal, and to kill, and to destroy: I am come that they might have life, and that they might have it more abundantly." This is the time that we must wax stronger and stronger in our level of faith. The Bible reads in **I John 4:4,** "Ye are of God, little children, and have overcome them: because greater is he that is in you, than he that is in the world." We are faced with all types of terrorism and fear. But, don't panic in the problem, don't faint in adversity, don't surrender in the flood, don't give up in the storm. Get past the pains of the past and stop crying over yesterday's disappointments. Be a warrior, not a whiner. GOD is on your side. You can choose to be pitiful or powerful. Stop mourning over things you cannot change. When the going gets tough, the tough should get going. Do what it takes to revive your faith. Stop allowing people to beat you down mentally. Develop some backbone. Avoid the catastrophe of negative conversation. Pick your self up from where you put yourself down. Stop allowing your mind to run away with negative thoughts. Learn how to overcome life's disappointments. Letting go of the past is a must in this last hour. Release it and let it go, whatever it is. Who wants self-pity? All that does is keep a chip on your shoulder.

Don't get stuck where you are. Always know that when one door closes, two doors open. Stop being hard and critical of yourself. Stop trying to fix something that you know cannot be fixed. This is the necessity of, **"If You Can Look Up, You Can Get Up!"** This book is designed to help change your life and set you back on target with a life of "victory."

One thing about GOD is that He always has a bigger plan. **Jeremiah 29:11 reads,** *"For I know the thoughts that I think toward you, saith the LORD, thoughts of peace, and not of evil, to give you an expected end."* The more you dwell on the past, the more you block your future. Until you let go of the old, you will never receive the new. It is time to start trusting GOD in times of trouble. Jesus says in **St. John 16:33**, *"In the world ye shall have tribulation: But be of good cheer; I have overcome the world."* Don't allow your present trouble to turn you away from GOD or the church. The church is a haven of rest. Shepherds are designed to watch over your soul. Everybody, everywhere, every age and every color faces life's troubles. You are either on your way into trouble, in the middle of trouble, or coming out of trouble. No one is exempted from trouble, but "Trouble don't last always!"

In **Philippians 4:7** the Bible reads, *"And the peace of God, which passeth all understanding, shall keep your hearts and minds through Christ Jesus."* The Bible reads in **Romans 8:35,** *"Who shall separate us from the love of Christ? Shall tribulation, or distress, or persecution, or famine, or nakedness, or peril, or sword?"* The Bible reads in **St. John 16:24,** *"Hitherto have ye asked nothing in my name; ask, and ye shall receive that your joy may be full."* The Bible reads in **Revelation 3:21,** *"To him that overcometh will I grant to sit with me in my throne, even as I also overcame, and am set down with my Father in his throne."*

So, as you can see, we all face hot spots in life. Noah faced mocking when he was told to build the Ark. Abraham faced mocking when he was told to offer his only son Isaac as an offering to GOD. Joseph faced prison. Moses faced the Red Sea. David faced Saul's attempts to kill him 21 times. Job faced great loss. Daniel faced the Lion's den. The Hebrew boys faced the fiery furnace. Stephen faced stoning. Paul faced shipwreck. Jesus faced the cross. So, what makes you and I any different?

When facing troubles of any kind, make sure you are not the cause. Many people are the cause of their own hardship through that foul spirit of disobedience to GOD, our Creator. When we disobey GOD, we set ourselves up for shipwreck. We must be aware of the "Jonah" spirit. We must follow GOD and quit questioning Him. Don't forget when we face trouble it does not mean we

"If You Can Look Up, You Can Get Up!"

are out of GOD's will. Remember, GOD is always on our side in good times and bad.

Life gives lemons at times, but let GOD's power show through you in the midst of sour situations. Let GOD's power show through you in the midst of good or bad times, no matter what you face. Know that the storms are in our lives and they are there to meet the needs of other people. Many of the storms we face in our lives are only a test to be able to rescue them that face the same opposition. Turn what you face totally into the hands of GOD. Develop an unshakable confidence in GOD. Don't worry about anything. PRAY about everything. It's good to prepare for conflict but know that the victory comes from GOD. The Bible says in **Ephesians 6:10-11,** *"Finally my brethren, be strong in the Lord, and in the power of his might. Put on the whole armor of God, that ye may be able to stand against the wiles of the devil."*

This is your day for victory. Get your praise "*on*." Know that the praise burns the ears of the devil!!! Begin to turn your obstacles into opportunities, and know that your tomorrow is better than your today!!!

In your spare time I would like for you to read **Romans 8:28, I John 4:4, St. Luke 10:19, Isaiah 54:17, Daniel 11:32, and St. John 10:10.** These scriptures will begin to enlarge your vision in testing time. When we equip ourselves with the word of GOD, we put on the whole armor of GOD, and we develop the mentality of the warrior's mind set. See yourself breaking down barriers in your life. See yourself over the top. See yourself overcoming past failures. See yourself overcoming breakdowns. See yourself debt free. See yourself healed. See yourself prospering. See yourself renewing your youth. See yourself developing stronger and stronger. Begin to see yourself outside your box.

Take the limit off of GOD. See GOD as bigness in your life. See GOD as handling your impossibilities. GOD says believe Him for bigger things. Go beyond limited thinking. We know that limited thinking is "Stinking Thinking." GOD will go out of His way to get a miracle to you. He will cross a million people to spot you out. **Ephesians 3:20** reads, *"Now unto him who is able to do exceeding abundantly above all that we ask or think, according to the power that worketh in us."* Read these as inspiration: **St. Luke 5:4, Ephesians 3:20, and St. Luke 1:34.** As I said before in this book, "If You Can Look Up, You Can Get Up" Never, never, never lose hope in GOD. The Bible reads in **I Timothy 6:12,** *"Fight the good fight of faith, lay hold on eternal life, whereunto thou art also called, and hast professed a good profession before many witnesses."* Hope means to wish for something with expectation. It is to look forward with confidence. The Bible reads in **Hebrews 10:35,** *"Cast not away therefore your confidence, which hath great recompense of reward."* I find hope is all a man and woman have. Life is a fight. We fight despair, despondency, weariness, hopelessness, defeats, etc. So we need hope because our hope turns into faith. Hope is the wings of faith. GOD is the GOD of hope and comfort. As long as GOD is alive, and He is alive and well, there is always hope for His people. So we should live GOD's best for our lives. I find the focus for faith is upward. We must **"look up"** no matter what we face or how bad it looks.

Look what David said in **Psalm 121:1-2,** *"I will lift up mine eyes unto the hills, from whence cometh my help. My help cometh from the LORD, which made heaven and earth."* In the midst of David's adversity, he set his eyes on the most high GOD, who is in the highest place. He overcame all of life's circumstances, casualties, disappointments and frustrations. We magnify what we dwell on. The bigger we make GOD, the smaller the problem becomes. We serve the great **I AM;** there is no time for losing hope. Stay in the ring; refuse to be knocked out. Grab your smelling salt and live!

Paul said in **I Thessalonians 4:13,** *"That ye sorrow not, even as others, which have no hope."* **Romans 5:5** reads, *"And hope maketh not ashamed."* **Hebrews 11:1** reads, *"Now faith is the substance of things hoped for."* ***St. John 16:33*** reads, *"In the world ye shall have tribulation: but be of good cheer: I have overcome the world."* **I Corinthians 15:57** reads, *"But thanks be to God, which giveth us the victory through our Lord Jesus Christ."*

Now do you see why I never, never, never lose hope? We have far more for us than against us because we have GOD. When we have GOD we are not the minority; we are the majority. Paul says in **Romans 8:37,** *"Nay, in all these things we are more than conquerors through him that loved us."* **Isaiah 54:17** reads, *"No weapon that is formed against thee shall prosper; and every tongue that shall rise against thee in judgment thou shalt condemn."* Move from your place of "defeat," dry your tears, get your joy back, get back in the race, and put your boots back on. Do you know you have the blood of Jesus on your side?" We have all it takes to win the battles we face each day. **Ephesians 6:13** reads, *"Wherefore, take unto you the whole armor of God that ye may be able to withstand in the evil day, and having done all, to stand."*

Romans 8:31 reads, *"If God be for us, who can be against us?"* **Romans 8:28** reads, *"And we know that all things work together for good to them that love God."*

In your inspirational time, read **St. Luke 18:27** and **Ephesians 3:20.** As you can see, my forte is the word of GOD. The irony of the whole thing is that GOD is first no matter what. We should not be feeling sad, or lonely or melancholy all because of feeling deserted or abandoned. Let's not negate the fact that the WORD is real. We must stay agreeable and pleasant toward GOD. After all, you have only just a minute, only 60 seconds in it. *"Forced upon you, can't refuse it. Didn't seek it, didn't choose it. But, it's up to you to use it. You must suffer if you lose it. Give an account if you abuse it. Just a tiny little minute, but an eternity is in it."*

"If You Can Look Up, You Can Get Up!"

Quoted from Dr. Benjamin Mays

Let's begin our journey of blissful living. After all, **Proverbs 17:22** says, *"A merry heart doeth good like a medicine."* I have always said to expect GOD's presence. Stay alert to His voice. The need for the Holy Spirit is so vital in these end times. That's why we must stay set for miracles. I tell people all of the time, "Don't lose focus on eternal life. It's time for the truth." The main ingredient is the word of GOD. We must always expect answers to our prayers. So keep the faith and begin to change your appetite towards the things of GOD; because there is power in the blood of Jesus. But, remember success is walking in love. Did you know that your answer is on the way? Remember that GOD is a restorer. No matter what you have lost in life, no matter what Satan has robbed from you or your past, you can get it all back!

In your spare time read **Joel 2:35.** The Bible reads in **James 5:16,** *"The effectual fervent prayer of a righteous man availeth much."* It is what GOD says to your heart that counts. Ask GOD to turn it around for you one more time. **Job** said in **Chapter 14, verse 14,** *"All the days of my appointed time will I wait, till my change come!"*

Are you the cause of disarray and blunders in your life? Are you the cause of distractions and wrong choices in your life? Are you the cause of past mistakes and misused wisdom? Are you the cause of disadvantages you face and present circumstances? Are you the cause of your lack of resource and despondency? Are you the cause of your difficulties and depression? Are you the cause of your decomposing attitude? Are you the cause of your hardships and frustrations? If not, then line up your words and back them up with faith and begin to win. Know the power and the value of words. Words are creators. Begin to speak life and faith over your circumstances. Begin to prophesy your future. Prophesy victory over your life. Prophesy to those dead dreams, those dry bones, Red Seas, lion's dens, and Lazarus situations. God says in **Isaiah 57:19,** "I create the fruit of the lips." **Proverbs 18:21** reads, *"Death and life are in the power of the tongue; and they that love it shall eat the fruit thereof.*

Let's not lose the faith! Ladies and gentlemen, always remember, *Eve* lost the faith with disobedience. *Moses* lost the faith being a people pleaser. *Aaron* lost the faith making a false god. *Miriam* lost the faith making mockery of the prophet. *Elijah* lost the faith hiding from Jezebel. *Samson* lost the faith with Delilah. *David* lost the faith with Bathsheba. *Abraham* lost the faith with Hagar. *Saul* lost the faith with the witch of En-dor. *Job* lost the faith with hardship. *Akan* lost the faith as a thief. *Peter* lost the faith with cursing. *Jeremiah* lost the faith hiding in a dungeon. *Ananias* and *Sapphira* lost the faith lying to the Holy Spirit. *Thomas* lost the faith by doubting the resurrection. Don't you lose the faith. I know it's "tuff " at times, I know it gets hard in everyday life, but it's not over until you win! So, don't lose the faith!

Judas lost the faith by selling out his Savior. I always say, *"Play with the bees and you'll get stung," "Play with fire and you'll get burned, "Tease a pit bull and you'll be bitten," "Strike a snake and he'll strike back," "Give a mouse a cookie and he'll want milk." "Give the devil an inch and he'll take a mile."* Paul said in **Ephesians 4:27,** *"Neither give place to the devil."* **Ephesians 6:11,** *"Put on the whole armour of God, that ye may be able to stand against the wiles of the devil (6:13) and having done all, to stand (6:14) Stand therefore."* **Colossians 2:21** reads, *"Touch not; taste not; handle not."* **James 4:7 reads,** *"Submit yourselves therefore to God. Resist the devil, and he will flee from you."* **1 Peter 5:9** reads, *"Whom resist steadfast in the faith, knowing that the same afflictions are accomplished in your brethren that are in the world."* **I John 5:4** reads, *"For whatsoever is born of God overcometh the world: and this is the victory that overcometh the world, even our faith."* Did you know that the Word can keep you in any situation? Whatever we face in life, all of life's dilemmas, frustrations, circumstances, or roadblocks – the Word is there for us. David said in **Psalm 119:105,** *"Thy word is a lamp unto my feet, and a light unto my path."*

The world we live in needs the word of GOD so badly. Eighty percent of our United States faces some type of mental problem. One million are addicted every night to some sort of sleeping pill. Fifty-five percent of our nation is under suicide watch. This is why I say it is time for a change, for the better. So, life brought you a setback. Get back up and win! Discover what drives you. It is not so much what you are driving, but what is driving you. Drop what holds you back. It is time to maximize your potential in life. Begin to live the life you have always desired or dreamed about. You were born rich in the eyes of GOD. GOD declares us royal because of His royal blood. Begin to create abundance in every area of your life. You and I are true winners. Regardless of what we feel or face, we have been declared true winners. We can break through any limitations and get on with life. It is time to turn all resentments and anger into love. We must begin to make peace. It is all about achieving victories in life. But, we must walk in love. According to **Galatians 5:6,** *"For in Jesus Christ neither circumcision availeth anything, nor uncircumcision, but faith which worketh by love."*

So ask yourself, what is it that keeps me from getting GOD's best in my life. Let's start by getting focused and sound. Start by avoiding distractions in life. See unlimited wealth reaching out to you at all times. It is time for more in the future than you had in the past. Remember what I have said, "There is no power in panic." I have found that panicky people are cowardly people. Begin to develop the mind-set of coming out whatever storm you are in and see your way out. Set goals that will bring freedom to your life. Begin to do what you love. Turn all your negative thinking into positive energy. In other words, use momentum power. Make the right moves, the right decisions and keep the right focus at all times. **Galatians 5:1** reads, *"Stand fast, therefore, in the liberty wherewith Christ hath made us free, and be not entangled again with the yoke of bondage."* **Hebrews 11:6** reads, *"But without faith it is impossible to please him; for he that cometh to God must believe that he is and that he is a rewarder of them that diligently seek him."* **Isaiah 26:3** reads, *"Thou wilt keep him in perfect peace, whose mind is stayed on thee, because he trusteth in thee."* **Philippians 4:13** reads, *"I can do all things through Christ, who strengthen me."* **Romans 8:37** reads, *"Nay, in all these things we are more than conquerors through him that loved us."*

You are now standing at the brink of a comeback. I know life has tossed you a storm. I know life tossed you a roadblock, but the very moment you picked up this book you came to another horizon in your life. Have big dreams and do them, stop daydreaming. Take action and break all self-destructive habits and curses from your life. Start committing yourself to daily improvements. Become more courageous and live everyday with passion. Develop a hunger for the things of GOD because the best things of GOD are waiting for you. Defuse your stress level. Cause that blood pressure to go back down by getting back on a proper eating diet. You must now live no matter what. You have work to do and know that no one can take your place. It's up to you to make it happen. Get on an exercise regiment so that you can begin to live. Your best days are ahead! **Psalm**

91:16 encourages us: *"With long life will I satisfy him, and show him my salvation."*

I told you that things happen in life. Begin to see all of your challenges as opportunities. Now is the time to begin our wonderful world of faith and motivation in the next pages of this book. We have total victory over Satan. Remember, take one day at a time. I often say, "Inch by inch anything becomes a cinch." You can never just read this book and put it down. You will find yourself reading and re-reading it on a daily basis. This book is not a substitute for your Bible. The Bible is the number one book that helps change lives all over this nation. Your Bible is your first love. It is the recognized book for deliverance. However, **"If You Can Look Up, You Can Get Up"** is to help you in your daily walk, so, don't rush, take it a day at a time. Watch GOD move in your life. Watch all of those roadblocks come crashing down. Watch all those trenches and foxholes that have been set as ambush against you come crashing down. Your best days are ahead!

You will begin to see change in your mental status, your physical status, your spiritual status and everything about the triune man. Every part of you will begin to see change. Often we pray for GOD to make changes in our lives., but I have witnessed that when we change, automatically the climate changes. So, let's begin. Let's begin to develop a new horizon. Let's reach out and take the things the enemy said that we could not have. Listen; did you know that GOD has called you as an entrepreneur? GOD has called you to be the CEO, Chief Executive Officer, over every phase of your life. You are your own entrepreneur and you are the caretaker of your body. The responsibility of your spiritual life lies in you. GOD has declared you and me to reach the levels of high achievement in every walk of life.

This is going to be a great and exciting time!

CHAPTER II
Leap of Faith

For verily I say unto you, that whosoever shall say unto this mountain, Be thou removed, and be cast unto the sea; and shall not doubt in his heart, but shall believe that those things which he saith shall came to pass, he shall have whatever he saith. Therefore, I say unto you, Whatsoever, things ye desire, when ye pray, believe that ye receive them, and ye shall have them."
Mark 11:23-24

It's going to take a "leap" of faith to survive this jungle world we live in.

We must jump start our faith level to a higher ground. There are multiple streams of opportunities in life where we can continuously have breakthrough after breakthrough while enjoying life's best. But only faith in God's Word can make that possible. God can give us new ideas in His word. The information in GOD's word is priceless - outstandingly priceless. I have found some of my greatest breakthroughs have been because of in-depth study of the word. I have learned how to use the strategies of GOD by investing in rich study time. That's what staying on the fast track is all about.

The Bible says in **Romans 10:8,** "But what saith it? The word is nigh thee, even in they mouth and in thy heart; that is, the word of faith, which we preach." Let's capitalize on the word "faith." The word "faith" is extremely powerful for our everyday walk here on earth. Know that our positive emotions trigger faith to fulfill achievements we've long waited for. In life there are stages before building our fortune. A miracle mind-set only comes by the word of GOD. It's time to find your source of power and that's word power. So banish doubt, negativity, and unbelief and start manifesting your destiny.

Let me give you some scriptural principles pertaining to GOD's word. When we start harnessing GOD's word, limitations disappear, and we begin to create our world the way we really want it to be. We need to be serious about a higher awareness. It's time to remove everyday irritations and worries from life. Let's replace stress with faith and begin a new sense of freedom. Let's look at the power of the word. **Proverbs 30:5 says,** *"The word of God is pure."* **Isaiah 40:8 says**, *"The Word of God shall stand forever."* **Luke 8:11 says,** *"The seed is the word of God."* **Hebrews 4:12** says, *"The word of God is quick and powerful."* We're talking about a leap of faith. Faith means "a confident belief in the truth" and "belief that does not rest on logical proof or material evidence." Let's see what the word says about faith because it's time out being grounded by the devil. It's time to elevate to a higher level of living. Recognize the strength you hold within. "Possession" is waiting on you. Start finding abundance in your life. Learn to avoid inner turmoil. Keep a quiet mind.

Follow your bliss and escape life's limits in order to achieve higher levels of happiness and success. Gain a new focus on life and create the awakened life. The Bible says in **I John 5:4,** *"This is the victory that overcometh the world, even our faith."* **James 2:17 says,** *"Faith without works is dead."* **Hebrews 11:6 says,** *"Without faith it is impossible to please Him."* **Galatians 5:6 says,** *"Faith which worketh by love."* **II Corinthians 5:7 says,** *"We walk by faith, not by sight."*

Galatians 2:20 says, *"I live by the faith of the Son of God."* **Romans 10:17 says,** *"So then faith cometh by hearing."* Faith is not something you stumble upon in the dark. Faith is the blueprint for your success. We can begin to tailor make our lifestyle. Let's begin to make it happen. Let's reinforce our dreams. Let's start building credibility principles regardless of the warfare. GOD wants His people, you and me, to begin goal-setting strategies that will put us over the top. Let's begin overcoming procrastination and begin increasing productivity. This will give us freedom, pure joy, and creativity. It's time for "spiritual growth" so eliminate fears and other obstacles. Start choosing positive thoughts and repeating affirmations to enrich relationships, embrace self-esteem, and transform your life.

Romans 12:1-2 says, *"I beseech you therefore, brethren, by the mercies of God, that ye present your bodies a living sacrifice, holy, acceptable unto God, which is your reasonable service. And be not conformed to this world, but be ye transformed by the renewing*

of your mind, that ye may prove what is that good, and acceptable, and perfect, will of God." **Achieve a healthy spirit, soul, and body. I Thessalonians 5:23 reads,** *"And the very God of peace sanctify you wholly; and I pray God your whole spirit and soul and body be preserved blameless unto the coming of our Lord Jesus Christ."* **Start living with purpose and passion. Begin to move your mountains and take your land.**
Matthew 17:20 reads, *"And Jesus said unto them, Because of your unbelief; for verily I say unto you, If ye have faith as a grain of mustard seed, ye shall say unto this mountain, Remove from here to yonder place; and it shall remove; and nothing shall be impossible unto you."* **Joshua 1:3 reads,**
"Every place that the sole of your foot shall tread upon, that have I given unto you, as I said unto Moses." Now do you understand "leap of faith"? Faith is leaping into GOD's word and standing strong no matter what, and learning to experience fulfillment and meaning to life. Remember, we're eliminating stress, worry, guilt, fear, depression, addictions, and other mental states that rob energy. Begin to transform your life and nourish your spirit to create wellness. Harness the limitless power of the word of GOD that will change your very life! Meditation is so important in this 21st century. **Joshua 1:8** tells us, "This book of the law shall not depart out of thy mouth, but thou shalt meditate therein day and night, that thou mayest observe to do according to all that is written therein." There's an art to success. **Matthew 6:33**

commands, "But seek ye first the kingdom of God, and his righteousness, and all these things shall be added unto you." Begin to take charge of your life! Ask yourself the question, "How hungry am I?" The word of GOD is number one. Cultivate unshakable character. Know that you are a natural champion, and that good things happen to people who believe in themselves. But you must be hungry! Start building your self-esteem. Avoid the pitfalls of negaholics, energy drainers, joy busters, and toxic people. Pinpoint specific areas in your life that need improvement and make positive changes right away. Nobody can push you as far as you can push yourself. This is a cutting-edge, goal achievement world in spite of economic conditions **(September 11, 2001.)** So tap into your deepest and most personal resources, the Holy Scriptures. Become all that you truly desire and deserve. When you begin to claim the abundant rewards your future has in store, you'll not only make a remarkable improvement in your life - but consequently in your world.

"Unleash the power within." Jude 24 reads, "Now unto him that is able to keep you from falling, and to present you faultless before the presence of his glory with exceeding joy." Begin celebrating your strengths and affirming your successes. Build your personal growth. Take the quantum - leap. Start keeping the promises you make to yourself. Stop manipulating yourself and arm yourself against the self-defeating effects of negative encounters. Start developing self-confidence.

Power speak yourself to day-to-day victories. **Proverbs 18:21** reads, "Death and life are in the power of the tongue, and they that love it shall eat the fruit thereof." **Proverbs 6:2** reads, "Thou art snared with the words of thy mouth, thou art taken with the words of thy mouth." Maintain a winning attitude. Build good habits and good relationships. Begin to advance to a whole new level of happiness and achieve and maintain a more peaceful state of mind. GOD wants His people mentally fit, energized, powerful and uplifting no matter what they face in life.

It seems in this 21st century people are looking for relationships instead of "responsibilities." People are not prioritizing values, or managing stress, or overcoming bad habits. Yet, they want total success and to become financially free. That's why we should stay mentally fit at all times. God has a step-by-step system in His word that will ignite the mind. **Philippians 4:8 reads,** "Finally, brethren, whatsoever things are true, whatsoever things are honest, whatsoever things are just, whatsoever things are pure, whatsoever things are lovely, whatsoever things are of good report; if there be any virtue, and if there be any praise, think on these things." One thing about the word of GOD is that it gives us astounding breakthroughs and helps us to overcome defeating fatigue and sluggishness when it comes to spiritual things.

High performance should be our endeavor. Creating your future allows you to identify and eliminate the most common roadblocks to enjoying peace of mind. Discover a new level of well being for yourself. Get back in touch with your dreams, move from fear to power. Overcome unhealthy beliefs and start back controlling your emotions. Know that you are too blessed to be stressed. Someone said he failed in business in 1831. He was defeated for state legislator in 1832. He tried another business in 1833. It failed. His fiancee died in 1835. He had a nervous breakdown in 1836. In 1843 he ran for congress and was defeated. He tried again in 1848 and was defeated again. He tried running for the Senate in 1855. He lost. The next year he ran for vice president and lost. In 1858 he ran for the Senate again and was defeated again. "Finally," in 1860, Abraham Lincoln was elected the 16th president of the United States. God will give you "double" for your trouble.

In **Job 42:12-13** we find that Job went from 7,000 sheep to 14,000, from 3,000 camels to 6,000, from 500 yoke of oxen to 1,000, from 500 she asses to 1,000 she asses - Praise God for the restoring God!!! **Joel 2:25-26** promises, *"And I will restore to you the years that the locust hath eaten, the cankerworm, and the caterpillar, and the palmer worm, my great army which I sent among you. And ye shall eat in plenty, and be satisfied, and praise the name of the Lord, who hath dealt wondrously with you; and my people shall never be ashamed."* Now let's begin a 31 day walk of blissfulness. Know that your best is yet to come no matter what you see. **"Pressure makes diamonds."** So let's become God's diamonds in the rough of life and begin to live each day in victory.

Day One

Only be thou strong and very courageous, that thou mayest observe to do according to all the law, which Moses, my servant, commanded thee: turn not from it to the right hand or to the left, that thou mayest prosper withersoever thou goest. 8) This book of the law shall not depart out of thy mouth; but thou shalt meditate therein day and night, and thou mayest observe to do according to all that is written therein: for then thou shalt make thy way prosperous, and then thou shalt have good success
(Joshua 1:7-8)

Doctor's Nuggets

What time is your thank you party?
God has zero tolerance for hate
Don't die until you're dead
Why keep making yourself a victim
No more falling and can't get up
Possess the winner's way
Input determines output
Get a new vision of life
Start building your (new) foundation
Attitude determines al-ti-tude
Enthusiasm makes the difference
Become the winner you were born to be
Let the past, be the past
Pull your own strings
There's a champion inside you
(See) yourself as a champion
The Word of God is the step to a champion mind set!
Take responsibility for your actions
Claim your healing and live!

"If You Can Look Up, You Can Get Up!"

Day Two

And I say also unto thee, that thou art Peter, and upon this rock I will build my church; and the gates of hell shall not prevail against it. 19) And I will give unto thee the keys of the kingdom of heaven: and whatsoever thou shalt bind on earth shall be bound in heaven: and whatsoever thou shalt loose on earth shall be loosed in heaven.
(St. Matthew 16:18-19)

Doctor's Nuggets

Celebrate yourself!!!
Know how to get anything you want
To G.E.T., you must A.S.K.
Start building winning relationships
Avoid toxic people
Use the power of faith
Avoid negaholics
Avoid energy drainers
Don't share your dream with a joy buster
Avoid "procrastination" and "procrastinators"
Set your opportunity clock, time is at hand
Avoid L.L.L. (Lack, Loss and Limitation)
Stay with O.Q.P. (Only Quality People)
Go back and live your dreams
Life is not a dress rehearsal, it's for real!
It's too soon to quit
Attitude...your greatest asset!!!
Trace it, face it, erase it and replace it!!
God has zero tolerance for sin!!!!
Claim your healing - Spirit, Soul and Body

Day Three

For which of you, intending to build a tower, sitteth not down first, and counteth the cost, whether he have sufficient to finish it?
(St. Luke 14:28)

Doctor's Nuggets

Don't start what you can't finish
Your what's to come is better than your what has been
The Word should be your waterfall of life!!
If you look down, you stay down
Who are you talking to?
Focus on being blissful
You "are" what you say!
You are who you are, and what you are, because of you!
Go from lemon to lemonade
If you can "see" it, you can "be" it
Dream, but don't daydream!
Don't be a copycat, be authentic
Your faith should be taking you somewhere!
Stop! Shoulda', Woulda', Coulda'
You have greatness in you!
So the sharks are in the ocean, So!
Don't wait for your ship, swim out and get it!
You can't defeat your giant with your mouth closed!

"If You Can Look Up, You Can Get Up!"

Day Four

"Behold, I give unto you power, to tread on serpents and scorpions, and over all the power of the enemy: and nothing shall by any means hurt you."
(St. Luke 10:19)

Doctor's Nuggets

Stay positive in a negative world!!
Take the "risk", swim with the sharks!
You can have it all (St. Matthew 6:33)
God has zero tolerance for sin
Your best days are ahead
"Yes" you can, and "Yes" you will
It's not over until you win!
How do you prioritize?
M.T.C. (Make Today Count)
Have a P.M.A. (Positive Mental Attitude)
Avoid Stinking Thinking!
Keep check ups, from the neck up
What do you say when you talk to yourself?
Feel the fear, but do it anyway!
Start spiritual growth
Start health and wealth building!
You must fight a war of words before you fight the actual battle!!!
Failure is only absolute when you give up!!!

Day Five

And the apostles said unto the Lord, Increase our faith. 6) And the Lord said, If ye had faith as a grain of mustard seed, ye might say unto this Sycamine tree, be thou plucked up by the root, and be thou planted in the sea; and it should obey you."
(St. Luke 17:5-6)

Doctor's Nuggets

Find the brightness in your problems...

Stop letting your present circumstances dictate your future!

Everything in life is up to you

You've been sitting down, laying down, and bowing down to

the devil long enough!

You are who you are, and where you are, and what you are,

because of your mouth!

Your what's going to happen, is better than your what's going on

Sink or Swim

Arise or Perish

Start the turning point

You can make it happen

Give a mouse a cookie, he'll want milk

Give the devil an inch; he'll take a mile

Only the strong survive

Start overcoming tough times

You are what you eat

You may be hindered, but refuse to be stopped!

Whoever wins the war of words will win the actual battle!

Day Six

"I can do all things through Christ which strengtheneth me."

(Philippians 4:13)

Doctor's Nuggets

Get rid of unpleasant, complaining, unforgiving people!
Stop letting small things seem big!
Winners stay with the "Word"
Average is an "enemy"
Im-itation is Lim-itation
Procrastination never grows
Stop living a double life. Negative/Positive
If you chase "two" rabbits, both will escape!
Line up "one" duck at a time
There is no future in the past
Do what people say cannot be done
The only place to start is where you are
Some "adversity" has advantages
Your best days are ahead!
Motivation is your key to victory
Start breaking down "barriers"
Be all you can be!
Be a winner in life!!!
Intense desire and belief can overcome the odds!!!

Day Seven

"For I am persuaded, that neither death, nor life, nor angels, nor principalities, nor powers, nor things present, nor things to come."
(Romans 8:38)

Doctor's Nuggets

Remember again pressure makes diamonds!
Avoid "distractions"
Stop giving in to the devil!
Become "totally" positive
Avoid "co-dependence"
Start using "confidence"
Start conquering fear & anxiety
"Create" your success
Find new "ecstasy" (Joy)!
Your past is NOT your future
"Invest" in yourself
Your "pain" can become your gain
Manage to survive trouble
"Conversation" reveals you!
Your tongue can open or close your door!
A positive attitude is the way of life
Seek out winners and overcomers
What's your attitude?

"If You Can Look Up, You Can Get Up!"

Day Eight

"Ask and it shall be given you; seek, and ye shall find; knock, and it shall be opened unto you: 8) for every one that asketh receiveth; and he that seeketh findeth; and to him that knocketh it shall be opened.
(St. Matthew 7:7-8)

Doctor's Nuggets

Worries, struggles, and fear must leave you!!!
You are the C.E.O. of your own life!
Turn those setbacks into comebacks, change/lanes!
If God's first, you're not last!
Too blessed, to be stressed
Claim your land for life
Rule #1: "Watch and Pray"
You must "see" it first
Unlock your "lock"
Get back in the ring
Why quit? The ship's coming!
Your 24 hours have started
No more "humpty-dumpty"
Start making healthy choices
Start taming your tongue
Get past scrambled eggs
Medium rare or well done
Your tomorrow is in your "mouth!"
On today I know I can survive!!!
Winners always do the right thing!!!
We become what we think!!!

Day Nine

"For I know nothing by myself; yet am I not hereby justified: but he that judgeth me is the Lord."
(I Corinthians 4:4)

Doctor's Nuggets

It's time to know your God!!!
You need to go to a P.M.A.P. (Positive Mental Attitude Party)
Quitting is not in my blood!
Don't just dream it, work it!
Persistence pays
Suicide is no option
Winners put faith in action
Living a double life will get you nowhere
"Unprofitable" is not for you
Get ahead of "self"
Success belongs to the "enthusiastic"
Have the courage to live, anyone can quit
Keep your temper, no one else wants it!
Do what people say cannot be done
Never take the advice of your fears
Do what's right
Be what you are
Don't jump into trouble "mouth" first!
I've got peace all around me!!!
All eagles were born to soar!!!

"If You Can Look Up, You Can Get Up!"

Day Ten

No weapon that is formed against thee shall prosper; and every tongue that shall rise against thee in judgment thou shalt condemn. This is the heritage of the servants of the Lord, and their righteousness is of me, saith the Lord.
(Isaiah 54:17)

Doctor's Nuggets

Avoid the victim "vocabulary"
Don't sweat the small "stuff"
Stand for what's right!
Don't sit back and take what comes, make it happen!
What's your final word?
Spark your fuse
Fear wants you to run
You can go anywhere you want in God!
Decision determines destiny
Destiny delayed is the devil's delight!
When life gives you a lemon, give it back!
Let go of whatever makes you quit
"Foundation" building is "brick by brick"
Your attitude is everything
Your enthusiasm is "not" showing
Failure is an event, not a person!
Change "negative" into "positive"
A setback is a set up for your comeback!
Remain optimistic!

Day Eleven

"Ye are my friends, if ye do whatsoever I command. Henceforth I call you not servants, for the servant knoweth not what his lord doeth; but I have called you friends; for all things that I have heard of my Father I have made known unto you.
(St. John 15:14-15)

Doctor's Nuggets

"Assess" your atmosphere, choose negative or positive
Live in the present moment
Avoid lack of resources
Start changing your beliefs
Start getting back on track
Let that worry go
Listen to your "wake" up call
Start using positive thinking
No more U-turns in life
Develop and exciting new day
Keep straight and go right
The right mental attitude brings success
Avoid life's dead ends
Faith works wonders
"Only-one-way"
No fear of anything
Heaven - A one-way highway
Know how to reach your goal
Use the keys to excellence
P.U.S.H. no matter what!

"If You Can Look Up, You Can Get Up!"

Day Twelve

"Ye are of God, little children, and have overcome them: because greater is he that is in you, than he that is in the world."
(I John 4:4)

Doctor's Nuggets

Get rid of destructive words
It only takes a minute to change your life
Let positive thinking work for you
Do you have what it takes?
Believe that you can, and you can
Start getting built to last
Know how to have the joy of life
Start returning to the basics of faith
Learn how to handle problems successfully
It's time to make a change
Relax and live above tension
Seesaw days are over
Let mind power work for you
Prepare for sundown
Stand tall and control your life
Make positive thinking and successful living work
Find how to be at peace with yourself
Imagine a great future for yourself
Positive people, positive results!!!

Day Thirteen

"Who so keepeth his mouth and his tongue keepeth his soul from troubles."
(Proverbs 21:23)

Doctor's Nuggets

Pinpoint your next "comeback"
A setback is a setup, for a comeback
Take control of your time
Achieve your full potential
Learn how to relax!
Lighten up, and have fun
How's your "visualization" - (what do you see?)
Be a P.P.P. (Power Packed Person)
Where's your motivation?
Attitudes are contagious, how's yours?
Learn how to communicate: home, job, church, and business
Stop being a carbon copy
Do it now!
How's your "image" book?
Go from complaining to obtaining
Think big!
Life is not "luck!"
Turn your scars into stars

Day Fourteen

"A man's belly shall be satisfied with the fruit of his mouth; and with the increase of his lips shall he be filled. 21) Death and life are in the power of the tongue and they that love it shall eat the fruit thereof."
(Proverbs 18:20-21)

Doctor's Nuggets

Protect yourself from "Obnoxious" doubters
Keep the power of vision
First things first!
Increase your effectiveness
Avoid self-sabotaging
You have "genius"
Rule #1: Responsibility!
"You" can make a difference
Think "determination"
Think "commitment"
Use effort and set goals
"Go" after opportunity
Clean your attitude
You are what you "think"
You are what you "eat"
Be a winner, not a quitter
You are God's greatest miracle!
It's not what you drive; it's what's driving you!
Self-sabotage must go!
Stop letting your present circumstances dictate your future!!
What you say is what you get!!

Day Fifteen

"The thief cometh not but for to steal, and to kill, and to destroy: I am come that they might have life, and that they might have it more abundantly."
(St. John 10:10)

Doctor's Nuggets

If you're fighting big battles, get ready for big victories!

If you knew my past, you would understand my praise

It only takes a minute...to turn a setback into a comeback!

You've got what it takes!

Be an "I" can do it person

Be a "no" limit person

Use your "degree" action

Know how to conquer your fears

Reach for "peak" performance

Develop your "sixth" sense "faith"

Learn the power of prayer!

Think top performance

Learn how to forgive

Learn the power of laughter

Release yourself from "buzzards"

Unlock the stuck door!

Accept "winning"

Take your best shot!

It's mine and can't nobody take it

Pressure makes diamonds

Slow down and enjoy life's journey

Day Sixteen

"What shall we then say to these things? If God be for us, who can be against us? 32) He that spared not his own Son, but delivered him up for us all, how shalt he not with him also freely give us all things?"
(Romans 8:31-32)

Doctor's Nuggets

What do you see? Because what you see is what you get!
Attitude...your greatest asset
Control negative thinking
Turn obstacles into opportunities
Overcome self limiting beliefs
Learn to energize yourself and stay motivated
Gain mastery over unwanted habits
Is your attitude affecting your success in life?
Develop positive attitudes that will help you reach your goals
Eliminate negative thoughts that hold you back from success
Take back ownership
Negative thinking is detrimental
Practice maintaining a positive attitude
Start forming positive habits
What are you saying to yourself?
You are what you think
Take control and conquer your fears
Control the worry syndrome!
It's all "good!"

Day Seventeen

"When thou passest through the waters, I will be with thee; and through the rivers, they shall not overflow thee; when thou walkest through the fire, thou shalt not be burned; neither shall the flame kindle upon thee."
(Isaiah 43:2)

Doctor's Nuggets

"Contentious" people can be your "poison"

If the dream is big enough, the problem doesn't matter

You can't stay where you are, if there's somewhere else to go!

Go from regrets of the past, to dreams of the future

Go from frustrated to focused

Love Life and life will love you back

Start finding the greatest you!

Start using your personal power

Start building a foundation

Start improving today

Awaken to limitless possibilities

All the things you want in life, are yours for the asking

Start transforming your life!

Unleash the power within

Start breaking old patterns and destroy them

Condition yourself mentally

Create "non-staggering" faith!

"Harness" your anger!!

Day Eighteen
"Now unto him that is able to do exceeding abundantly above all that we ask or think, according to the power that worketh in us."
(Ephesians 3:20)

Doctor's Nuggets
If you knew my past, you would understand my praise!
It's time for a change for the better!
You've had a setback, now what?
Get your self-esteem back up and win!
Discover what drives you!
Drop what holds you back
Maximize your potential
Live the life you desire
You were born rich
Create abundance in every area of your life
You're a true winner
Break through any limitation and get on with your life
Turn resentment and anger into love (make peace)
Achieve "victories" in your life
What is it that keeps you from asking?
Keep your mind "focused" and "sound"
Avoid distractions (Lot's wife)
"See" unlimited wealth
It's time for more in the future, than you've had in the past

Day Nineteen

"The righteous cry, and the Lord heareth, and delivereth them out of all their troubles. 18) The Lord is nigh unto them that are of a broken heart; and saveth such as be of a contrite spirit. 19) Many are the afflictions of the righteous; but the Lord delivereth him out of them all."

(Psalms 34:17-19)

Doctor's Nuggets

Choose to stay happy!
There's no power in "panic"
Develop the mind set of coming "out"
Set goals that will bring freedom to your life
Do what you love!
Turn negative thinking into positive energy
Change your life
Use your momentum "power"
Make the right moves at the right time
You are standing at the brink of "comeback"
Have big dreams, and do them
Take action "now"
Break lifelong self-destructive habits
Commit yourself to "daily" improvement
Become more courageous
Live every day with "passion" (hunger)
Defuse your stress!
"Stuff" happens
1-800-brick-wall
What's next? (jump-over)
See challenges as opportunities!!!

Day Twenty

"Though I walk in the midst of trouble, thou wilt revive me; thou shalt stretch forth thine hand against the wrath of mine enemies, and thy right hand shall save me. 8) The Lord will perfect that which concerneth me: thy mercy, O Lord, endureth forever: Forsake not the works of thine own hands."
(Psalms 138:7-8)

Doctor's Nuggets

Be yourself, and live!!!!
Look at your "options"
Stop living "off" course
Go to the next level!
Erase negative thought patterns
Take a "big" look
Power-boost your faith
Overcome old barriers and limitations
Get breakthroughs in spirit, soul and body
Start living the life you've always dreamed
Ignite your joy!
"Laughter," a dose of the best medicine
Launch from defeat to victory
Your future is in your mouth
"Saying" is believing
Eliminate lifelong fears
Turn problems into stepping-stones!
Garbage in, garbage out!
Winners always "focus!"

Day Twenty-One

"Humble yourselves therefore under the mighty hand of God, that he may exalt you in due time. 7) Casting all your care upon him; for he careth for you. 8) Be sober, be vigilant; because your adversary the devil, as a roaring lion, walketh about, seeking whom he may devour."
(I Peter 5:6-8)

Doctor's Nuggets

Take life one day at a time
Quitting is not in my blood
Enhance your spiritual, mental and physical performance
Profit from the Word!
Take "impossible" steps
Discover how to recognize what you do best
Turbo charge your "faith"
Build self-esteem
Harness the power
Nurture your greatness
Be C.C.C. (Cool, Calm and Collected)
No "free" way to success
Start defeating fatigue and sluggishness
Turn stumbling blocks into building blocks
Start personal development
Stop letting your present circumstances dictate your future
Refuse to "feed" an argumentative spirit!!!!

"If You Can Look Up, You Can Get Up!"

Day Twenty-Two

"Neither do men light a candle, and put it under a bushel, but on a candlestick; and it giveth light unto all that are in the house. 16) Let your light so shine before men, that they may see your good works, and glorify your Father which is in heaven."
(St. Matthew 5:15-16)

Doctor's Nuggets

Sin can break your "focus!"
You can have lights, you can have cameras, but nothing happens
until you take action
Overcome limitations!
Discover the "secrets" of God's Word
Live enjoyable, productive and profitable
"See" achieving your goals
Start self-mastering discipline
Make the most of your personal, spiritual and professional life
We are total winners
The "Word," a great road map to success
Push as far as you can "go"
Take control of your thoughts
Overcome feelings of unworthiness
Set higher goals
Let your faith do the talking
Develop your own planning system
Master Your time!
A goal is a dream with a deadline
If you "stumble" don't stop!
You can make it!!!!

Day Twenty-Three

"Fear thou not; for I am with thee; be not dismayed for I am thy God: I will strengthen thee; yea I will help thee; yea, I will uphold thee with the right hand of my righteousness. For I the Lord thy God will hold thy right hand, saying unto thee, fear not; I will help thee."

(Isaiah 41:10 and 13)

Doctor's Nuggets

Re-direct your conversation to positive - power!!!!
Make a commitment to your commitment
Take lessons in achievements
Make winning a habit
Create focus
Start bouncing back from setbacks
Stay out of the "past"
Take charge of your life
Start attaining incredible success
Profit from the winner's way
"Fuel" your action with ambition
Convert fears into "burning" desires
Walk your talk straight to the top!
Maintain balance
Develop championship traits
Have your best year ever
Be with effective people!
Don't settle for less
Life's a trip, "live" it up!
Face your fires and fears

"If You Can Look Up, You Can Get Up!"

Day Twenty-Four

"Ask and it will be given you; seek and you shall find; knock and it shall be opened unto you. For everyone that asketh receiveth; and he who seeketh findeth; and to him that knocketh, it shall be opened."
(St Matthew 7:7-8)

Doctor's Nuggets

Identify "complainers" and cut them off!!!!
Affirm to win; refuse to lose
Endure great obstacles
Embrace principles that bring stability
Accomplish anything you want!
Gain "triumphs"
Make yourself more confident
Find yourself in greater control of your life
Always perform at your peak
Overcome "self-defeating" behaviors
Break the bonds of limited thinking
Start gaining personal development
Gain higher returns on your spiritual investments
Develop mind power
Banish time wasters
Don't be fooled by last year's warfare!
Start providing the tools to make it happen!
Heal the wounds of your past, so you don't continue to bleed
Looking ahead spells "victory"

Day Twenty-Five

"Yea, though I walk through the valley of the shadow of death, I will fear no evil; for thou art with me; thy rod and thy staff they comfort me. Thou preparest a table before me in the presence of mine enemies: thou anointest my head with oil; my cup runneth over. Surely goodness and mercy shall follow me all the days of my life: and I will dwell in the house of the Lord forever."

(Psalms 23:4-6)

Doctor's Nuggets

As you think, so are you!!
Stay on top in a changing world
Track down your goals
Attract profitable breakthroughs
New level, new devil!
Set your course with your tongue
"You" are the voice of faith'
Stop giving in to rejection
Pick up those "ugly" feelings
How saved is your mouth?
If God says you can, you can!
Don't give a "rip" how you feel!
You have divine favor
Cross your finish line
Advance to new heights
You are a "free" agent!
Pave your own road, and start walking!!!
Staying happy is a healthy "choice!!!!"
You are what you eat!!!!

"If You Can Look Up, You Can Get Up!"

Day Twenty-Six

"That at that time ye were without Christ, being aliens from the commonwealth of Israel, and strangers from the covenants of promise, having no hope, and without God in the world. 13) But now in Christ Jesus ye who sometimes were far off are made nigh by the blood of Christ. 14) For he is our peace, who hath made both one, and hath broken down the middle wall of partition between us."

(Ephesians 2:12-14)

Doctor's Nuggets

Your life is going to make you or break you!!!
Stop being a "frustrated" passenger in life!!!
Take a candid look at what it takes to survive
You cannot fail, victory is 100% guaranteed!
Be entrepreneurial minded, seek information
Fit the future to your life
Leap over personal obstacles, and brush aside fears
Don't pass up opportunities!
Boldness (+) Flexibility (=) Success
Keep thriving in chaos
Gain a renewed life, have vision and purpose
Accelerate your effectiveness
Meet and beat your fears
Boost yourself
Identify and understand your "niche"
Nurture the wisdom within
Laugh yourself well!
Kill all the "giants" because others are coming!
Learn how to keep joy, even when the bottom falls out

Day Twenty-Seven

"Thy shoes shall be iron and brass; and as thy days, so shall thy strength be. 26) There is none like unto the God of Jeshurun, who rideth upon the heaven in thy help, and in his excellency on the sky. 27) The eternal God is thy refuge, and underneath are the everlasting arms: and he shall thrust out the enemy from before thee; and shall say, destroy them.
(Deuteronomy 33:25-27)

Doctor's Nuggets

Some of you would receive your miracle if you would learn to have joy!!!!
Avoid comfort zones that yield to defeat!!!
We all have "turbulent" times!
Laughter can lower your blood pressure
In times of adversity "lighten up"
Gain a healthy new outlook on life
Start discovering new paths
Discard your doubts
Live life without any limits
Defuse any failure
Avoid negative "mind" programming
You're incredible!
End self-sabotage
Break through mental barriers to peak performance
The "Word" is priceless information
Gain "Zest" for your life
You have "inner" fire!
"Alone" is at the top!
A "No" is a "Yes" waiting to happen!
Who you linger with, becomes you!!!!

"If You Can Look Up, You Can Get Up!"

Day Twenty-Eight

"If ye abide in me, and my words abide in you, ye shall ask what ye will, and it shall be done unto you. 8) Herein is my Father glorified, that ye bear much fruit; so shall ye be my disciples. 9) As the Father hath loved me, so have I loved you: continue ye in my love."
(St. John 15:7-9)

Doctor's Nuggets

Avoid the D's - Despondency, Depression, and Defeat
Get "clarity" in your life
Unleash your "unlimited" potential
Start improving your self-discipline
Gain "uncompromising" commitment...to excellence
Benefit from the past and breakthrough to the future
Evaluate your own personality
Stop manipulating yourself
Set goals and reach them
Begin your jump to the top
Take a fascinating look at your victory
Stop worrying and start living
Avoid fatigue
Turn criticism to your advantage!
Do what works, do what matters
Discover how to control your life
Study the Word!
Life is not a playground, it's a battleground!
Stop dragging the "weight" of your past into your present!

Day Twenty-Nine

"And Caleb stilled the people before Moses, and said, Let us go up at once, and possess it, for we are well able to overcome it. 31) But the men that went up with him said, we be not able to go up against the people; for they are stronger than we. 32) And they brought up an evil report of the land which they had searched unto the children of Israel, saying, The land, through which we have gone to search it, is a land that eateth up the inhabitants thereof; and all the people that we saw in it are men of great stature. 33) And there we saw the giants, the sons of Anak, which come of the giants; and we were in our own sight as grasshoppers, and so we were in their sight."
(Numbers 13:30-33)

Doctor's Nuggets

Discover your driving force!!!
Success is step-by-step!
Attract and accumulate faith
Do what you love to do
Reach for prosperity, peace and health
Be financially free!
God made you one-of-a-kind
Overcome the day in - day out spirit
Control your "Word" flow
Take control of your attitude
Your thoughts and fears developed from early childhood
Get to the "root" of what holds you back
Discover how to defeat the devil
Replace poverty consciousness with prosperity consciousness
Are you hiding behind a mask?

"If You Can Look Up, You Can Get Up!"

Day Thirty

"Acquaint now thyself with him, and be at peace: thereby good shall come unto thee. 23) If thou return to the Almighty, thou shalt be built up, thou shalt put away iniquity far from the tabernacles. 24) Then shalt thou lay up gold as dust, and the gold of Ophir as the stones of the brooks."

(Job 22:21 and 23-24)

Doctor's Nuggets

Recognize a problem as a challenge!
Stop being a cookie cutter, be yourself!
Increase your intelligence; you'll need it!
Become proficient
Overcome phobias!
Develop "mega" memory in the Word
Develop "skill" building exercises
Discover the incredible you!
You have the power to find solutions
Learn to communicate powerfully, properly and effectively
Banish time wasting and procrastination
Improve your "Word" power
Create a powerful focus
Speak with power
Generate breakthrough ideas
Gain mastery over your defeats!
Break habits you've tried to change for years
Facing the fire is overcoming all negatives in life!!!
People don't like commitment, because commitment demands "change"
Eliminate self-sabotage!!!

Day Thirty-One

""Come now, and let us reason together, saith the Lord: though your sins be as scarlet, they shall be as white as snow; though they be red like crimson, they shall be as wool. 19) If ye be willing and obedient, ye shall eat the good of the land: 20) but if ye refuse and rebel, ye shall be devoured with the sword: for the mouth of the Lord hath spoken it."
(Isaiah 1:18-20)

Doctor's Nuggets

Lighten up and learn to laugh!!!
God wants his people free!
Banish all your doubts
Turn your every day actions into victory
Erase lifelong fears
Remove emotional conflicts
Create a "faith"…where everything is possible
Visualize your success
Overcome your mental roadblocks
Start creating everyday "miracles!"
Don't sweat the small stuff
Practice your love walk
Start developing your "sixth" sense "faith"
Use the power of prayer
Gain a life of heaven on earth
Find your keys for life's purpose!
Stop just going through the motions
We spend too much time worrying!!!
Stop dwelling on life's negatives
Connect with the winners!

Made in the USA
Lexington, KY
24 November 2016